# CELEBRATE·THE·WORLD

# Lunar New Year

By Hannah Eliot
Illustrated by Alina Chau
SCHOLASTIC INC.

On the first day of the Chinese calendar, the new moon is in the sky and the stars shine bright. It is time for a big celebration.

春節快樂

This festival is known
by many names:
**Chinese New Year**,
**Spring Festival**, and
**Lunar New Year**.
It marks the passage
of the harvest season
and celebrates the
coming spring.

Each new year is represented by one of twelve different animals of the Chinese zodiac.

The animals are: the rat, ox, tiger, rabbit, dragon, snake, horse, goat, monkey, rooster, dog, and pig.

Before the new year celebrations begin, we clean our homes—and ourselves! This symbolizes washing away anything bad from last year and starting fresh.

We feast and celebrate with our families because Lunar New Year is about preparing for good luck in the coming year, and it's also about family and honoring our ancestors.

Many of the holiday's traditions come from a very old tale. There is an ancient Chinese legend that tells of a monster named **Nian**, who had the head of a bull and the body of an ox. Once a year, Nian would come out of hiding and scare people.

But the monster was afraid of three things: the loud crackling of burning bamboo (or firecrackers), the color red, and the bright lights of lanterns.

Today, we light **baozhu**, or firecrackers, lanterns, and fireworks, and we hang red signs with blessings to keep Nian away.

Red symbolizes good luck. We also display other things that represent luck, such as the Chinese character **fu** (福), elaborate knots, and paper cuttings with beautiful words or pictures.

The Lunar New Year celebrations last fifteen
days. During the first days, we visit our friends
and family, and we stay up all night enjoying the
company of one another!

We eat dumplings filled with all sorts of delicious meats and vegetables.

Because the dumplings are shaped like **yuanbao**, an ancient kind of money, we hope that they will bring wealth and prosperity in the coming year.

Children also receive red envelopes with money from their parents, grandparents, and other family members, and friends. These are called **hongbao**.

This tradition comes from the legend of an evil spirit called **Sui**. Parents used to thread eight coins on a red string and place them under their children's pillows to protect them from the spirit.

On the fifteenth night, the full moon returns to the sky and we honor the end of Lunar New Year with the Lantern Festival.

We celebrate with parades led by people dressed
as dragons and lions. These animals bring us good
fortune and luck.

And we gather once more with our friends and family to eat sticky rice balls.

This special food is round like the full moon, and it reminds us to live the new year in harmony and happiness.

ISBN 978-1-338-54788-7

12 11 10 9 8 7 6 5 4 3 2 1               19 20 21 22 23 24

Printed in the U.S.A.                         40

First Scholastic printing, January 2019

Designed by Julie Robine